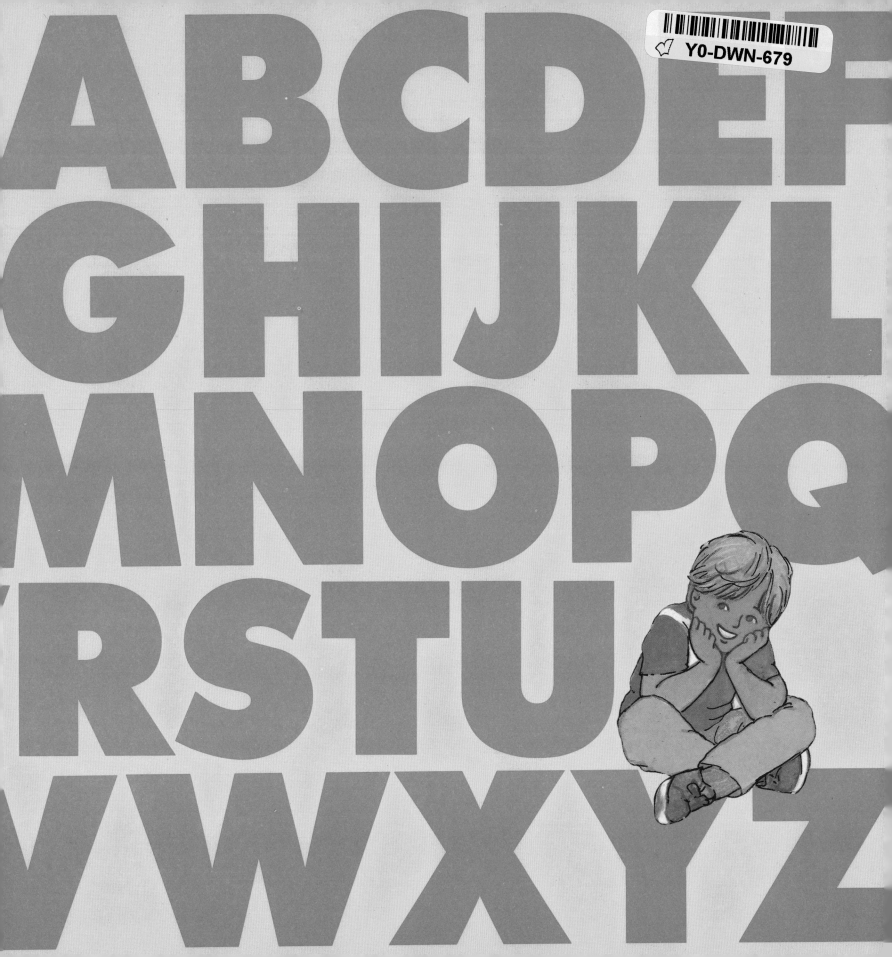

To Amanda Machen
from
Mary + Bob Sloge
Dec. 1999

Published by Modern Publishing
A Division of Unisystems, Inc.

Copyright © 1988 by Sally Masteller

TM – a Self-Discovery Book is a trademark owned by
Modern Publishing, a division of Unisystems, Inc.
All rights reserved.

® – Honey Bear Books is a trademark owned by
Honey Bear Productions, Inc., and is registered
in the U.S. Patent and Trademark Office.
All rights reserved.

No part of this book may be reproduced or copied
in any format without written permission from
the Publisher.

All Rights Reserved.

Printed in Italy

a Self-Discovery Book ™

Feelings A to Z

by Sally Masteller

Modern Publishing
A Division of Unisystems, Inc.
New York, New York 10022

Aa is for angry.

Bb is for brave.

Cc is for curious.

Dd is for disgusted.

Ee is for excited.

Ff is for frightened.

Gg is for glad.

Hh is for helpful.

Ii is for impatient.

Jj is for jealous.

Kk is for kind.

Ll is for lonely.

Mm is for merry.

Nn is for nervous.

Oo is for open.

Pp is for proud.

Qq is for quiet.

Rr is for rude.

Ss is for surprised.

Tt is for tender.

Uu is for useful.

Vv is for vital.

Ww is for wild.

Xx is for X-tra shy.

Yy is for youthful.

Zz is for ...

...**zonked!**